Poems Born in Bergen-Belsen

Poems Born in Bergen-Belsen

By

Menachem Z. Rosensaft

Cover design by Shay Culligan
Cover photography by Thomas Rahe
Back cover photograph by Shahar Azran

ISBN: 978-1-952326-54-7

Kelsay Books
502 South 1040 East, A-119
American Fork, Utah, 84003

For Hallie and Jacob

To bless grandchildren and be blessed by them, to teach them and to be taught by them—these are the highest Jewish privilege.
—Rabbi Lord Jonathan Sacks

Acknowledgments

I want to acknowledge the publications in which the following poems, some in earlier versions, previously appeared:

Blood to Remember, American Poets on the Holocaust (Charles Adés Fishman, Ed., Revised, second edition, Time Being Books, 2007): "Birkenau Barracks;" "The Second Generation" (also in *Midstream*);"Sosnowiec Visited" (also in *Rayonot: A Journal of Ideas*); "Yad Vashem Museum Opening"
The Hidden Child: "night fragments"
Jewish Heritage: "Kol Nidre in Bergen-Belsen" (also in *Witness to the Holocaust,* Azriel Eizenberg, Ed., The Pilgrim Press, 1981)
Jewish Spectator: "Thunder Burial;" "Mute Lamentations;" "Treblinka;" "I Believe"
The Jewish Quarterly (London): "Montage"
Midstream: "Kaddish" (also in *Rayonot: A Journal of Ideas*); "Crematory Smoke;" "Lamentations" (also in *Witness to the Holocaust*); "Midnight Hallucinations;" "Yizkor;" "Morning Prologue;" "Tishah b'Av, 1943;" "The Second Generation" (also in *Blood to Remember, American Poets on the Holocaust*); "Father" (also in *Mishkan T'filah, A Reform Siddur*);"voiceless melodies;" "Yearnings for My Father;" "Rain Mornings;" "Messianic Shadows;" "Genesis, Post Scriptum;" "Refugee;" "strange days follow wartime."
Mishkan T'filah, A Reform Siddur (Elyse D. Frishman, Ed., Central Conference of American Rabbis, 2007): "Father" (also in *Midstream*)
Rayonot: A Journal of Ideas (Park Avenue Synagogue, New York City): "they burn, the fires of the night;" "Kaddish Memories of My Mother;" "Sosnowiec Visited" (also in *Blood to Remember, American Poets on the Holocaust*); "A Legacy of Whispers"
Tablet: "Meditation on a Ghost Child"

Siddur Tishah B'Av (Rabbinical Assembly, 2003): "Poland" (also in *I Am Jewish, Personal Reflections Inspired by the Last Words of Daniel Pearl,* Judea and Ruth Pearl, Eds., Jewish Lights Publishing, 2004)

Visiting Scribes, The Jewish Book Council: "Auschwitz-Birkenau, January 27, 2015"

Gratitude

My teacher and mentor Elie Wiesel instilled in me a reverence for language and an awareness that words placed in their proper order can turn into burning scars. Throughout a friendship of more than five decades, he generously read and critiqued my poems and other writings. He also introduced me to Professor Elliott Coleman, the chairman of The Writing Seminars at Johns Hopkins University who gave me the confidence to discover my poetic voice.

I am deeply grateful to Karen Kelsay and her team at Kelsay Books for so sensitively transforming my 82 individual poems into the beautiful volume the reader now holds in their hands; to Evan Fox for graciously proofreading the manuscript; and to photographer extraordinaire Shahar Azran for formatting the cover photograph of the Jewish Monument at Bergen-Belsen.

The quote by the late Rabbi Lord Jonathan Sacks on the dedication page is from his video commentary on the weekly Torah portion *Vayechi*, produced by the office of the Chief Rabbi of the United Hebrew Congregations of the Commonwealth, 2010.

Nothing I have ever achieved, including the present book, would have been possible without Jeanie who has been and is my love, my best friend, my inspiration, and my sounding board. Jodi, Mike, Jacob, and Hallie are the reason for everything I write and do. This collection of poems is my gift and my legacy to them.

Contents

in the seconds after the truck hit me

in the seconds after the truck hit me
I know what it is
to almost die
to dread
not to be able to finish
all I've left to do
that I will never again kiss
my love
my best friend
hug my daughter
my grandchildren
wish friends a good morning
a good year
far too many thoughts
plans
dreams
converge
begin to fade
into black
and then
when the truck stops
my foot under its tire
I sense a soundless whisper
perhaps within me
perhaps from somewhere far away
telling me not today
not yet
but do not waste this gift
reprieve
this beginning of what could be
my next chapter
or my last

to our grandchildren in the time of Covid-19

alone
and yet connected to
you

alone
but able to see
        hear
you
on a laptop screen
iPad
iPhone

to be with
you
without being next to
you

laughing with
you
watching Hallie dance
listening to Jacob play his guitar
singing Shabbat prayers with
you
celebrating the Seder with
you
hugging
you
without touching
you

apart but still together

Baruch Atah Adonai Eloheinu

even in the time of Covid-19
we are blessed

Meditation on a Ghost Child

he
drifts aimlessly
through the snow
above the snow

the ghost child
does not know
who he is
who he was
if he was

he
does not speak
cannot speak
and because
he no longer knows
how to speak
refuses to speak

he
cannot understand
cannot recognize
cannot hear
words
laughter
screams

certainly not prayers

he
will not sanctify
glorify
forgive
curse

he
does not know how many
minutes, hours, days, weeks, months, years
he has drifted aimlessly
through the snow
above the snow
drenched by rain
scorched under an august sun
over grass
flowers
like the last flowers
he saw before
but always between
decaying
wooden walls

he
no longer remembers
a smile
a hug
a kiss

only faint echoes
of a lullaby

another ghost child walks
toward him
beside him

they
do not see each other
do not touch

no matter

they know they once
heard the same lullaby
became
the same ashes
dissipated into
the same grayness

two ghost children
drift aimlessly
through the snow
above the snow

they burn, the fires of the night

they burn, the fires of the night
exploding the sky's blackness
scorching heaven

the flames devour flesh
char bones
drink blood
each corpse reminding God
here is another Job
whose wealth You cannot replace
who will not have
seven more sons
and three more daughters

the flames silence prayers
shatter dreams
evaporate tears
each soul reminding God
here is another song
You will not hear again
You can never again create

they burn, the fires of the night
exploding the world's blackness
scorching us

Poland

I am the Jew
who would have prayed
three times a day
had black flames
not spewed me
into the August sky

without a grave
without a stone
my ashes
screams
burning blood
have penetrated
Carthage-like
this earth
that did not quake
to shatter crematory walls
that did not swallow
railroad tracks
whose grass refused
to become crimson

I know
of course I know
that all earth is innocent
only the killers
killed

I know
of course I know
that Germans
not Poles
murdered the I
I would have been

but covered by the dust
of that other I
and of all the millions
of other I's
even fields
where flowers never withered
have become desolation
devastation

they stood there watching
Staszek and Leszek
as I was shoved
into the cattle car
good riddance to the bloody Jews
they thought
we'll get their houses now
they thought

they stood there smiling
Hans and Fritz
as they shoved me
into the gas
good riddance to the bloody Jews
they thought
it's almost time to eat
they thought

I am the last Jew to die
there
the last Jew to die
the last Jew
I am

Psalm XXIII at Auschwitz

a psalm to the emptiness
no shepherd
only foes
no festive table
only bitter soup
moldy bread
no green pastures
no still waters
only blood-drenched
rat-infested
mud
he is always
hungry
she is always
cold
their heads anointed
by blows
shadows walking
through the valley of death
Adonai's fog-wrapped house
forever

You who sits in heaven

You who sits in heaven
hide Your eyes
as forever tortured souls
become immortal
in the shadow of charred bones
unpurged of their crucible
still reeking of zyklon-b
and only a hovering butterfly
born against lightning
above flowers
growing despite night
after night
reminds fire ghosts
that You
have once been here

A Refusal to Forgive the Death, by Gas, of a Child in Birkenau

whom should I forgive?
why should I forgive?
how can I forgive?

children

hundreds
of children

thousands
thousands upon thousands
of children

hundreds of thousands
of children

more than one million children

starved
beaten
typhus-ridden
shot
hanged
gassed

but I see
one child
only one child
always one child
always the same child

a five-and-a-half-year-old boy

Benjamin

my mother's son
my mother's child
his ashes diffused
toward the stars
almost three years
before I was born

once upon a time
my brother
used to laugh
used to play
used to sing
used to have
tomorrows

but that was before

before the train
before arrival
at a place
with a German name
before one last hug
one last kiss
before he went
with his father
and grandparents
into a blackness
without end

whom should I forgive?
why should I forgive?
how can I forgive?

and death now has its dominion

and death now has its dominion
not as a distant end
or unwelcome guest
but invited in
as full omnipresent companion
to comfort the still living
barely living

and death now has its dominion
as they scream in its shadow
see it claim mother after
brother after cousin after
sister after
uncle after neighbor after friend after
aunt after stranger
a holy congregation
of the damned and doomed

and death now has its dominion
receiving prayers not for God
who either would not listen
or could not hear
prayers for it
to wait
come now
be painless
be quick
please spare my mother
brother
cousin
sister
uncle
neighbor
friend

aunt
even the stranger

and death now has its dominion
like every true overlord
moving on inexorably
undeterred
not pausing to listen
hear
as corpses burn
souls merge into flames
ascending not toward any heaven
but into oblivion
above clouds

and death now has its dominion

l'aube du Christ

l'aube du Christ
d'un Christ
d'un autre Christ
d'un enfant
presque déjà oublié

bone-chilling
shadowless night
interrupted
by jarring flames
fades into
deeper black
in which dawn
any dawn
even a messianic dawn
especially a messianic dawn
is an impossibility
beyond redemption

screams
howls
gasping coughs
silences by the unspoken
deafening
j'accuse
of one
hundreds
of ones
thousands
hundreds of thousands
millions
of ones
echoing

in an already forgotten emptiness
where God does not dare
intrude

et c'est la vraie mort
du Christ
de l'autre Christ
d'une enfant
déjà oubliée

Selection: August 1943

snarling dogs drooling at the mouth
tear blood-soaked flesh
from a still breathing
still howling
almost carcass
sleep unbathed
fornicate
in their own urine
and are more God-like
than the spotlessly uniformed
Mozart humming Goethe quoting
oh so clean shaven and always polite
son of a hausfrau
M.D., Ph.D., Heidelberg, if you please
who inspects his prey
one after another after another
after another
with a bored smile
before dinner

Miserere: Psalm 55 in Counterpoint

returning in one final ice wind
not on doves' or eagles' wings
the messiah
real, false, imagined
and his father
both pale, both bearded, both frail
were immediately recognized as
racially impure
by an efficient aryan prototype
who knew his catechism

oh yes, I too refuse to mourn

oh yes, I too refuse to mourn
the death of a child
cast into immortality
of mankind's making

among weed-covered crumbling bricks
and rotting barracks
he plays with other shadows
invisible children like himself
while a frozen wind blows ashes
into melodies
only they can hear

he was born
I was born
our mothers hugged us
years apart
we turned one, then two, then four, then five
but he was never six years old
never was called to the Torah
never kissed a girl
never studied Ecclesiastes or Kierkegaard
never read Buber or Kafka
or even *The Little Prince*

unlike London's daughter
they did not feel the flames
that faded them as black clouds
into the synagogue of heaven
child souls

choking on their own now toxic breath
who did not suffer for God
for us
for any reason

oh yes, I too refuse to mourn

Psalm 102: Death Prayer

a prayer of the dead
from children's burning bones
drumbeat-cursed echo
against colliding hurricanes
indissoluble smoke
in the withered sanctuary where
abandoned by angels who witnessed
once uncorroded creation
You no longer hide Your face
And not even owls eat ashes any more

Psalm 121 On Fire

black eyes search for yesterday
above beyond walls
above beyond shadow fragments
above beyond imagined hills
search for human divine help
promised shelter
amid rags corpses vomit
"Mommy, are we going to live or die?"
his last words to our mother
but You
who would be my brother's guardian
be at his side on paths
he never got to walk
slumber
as the sun murders with Your heat
the moon with its indifference
sleep
while atonal melodies bereft of life
ascend from their depth
through charred skeletal trees
and one more five-year-old soul
shatters unprotected
into flames raging up
toward Your sky
Your stars
Your forever

Kaddish

hear the little children cry
    hear them scream
as they die
never will another sound
    echo through Your heart

muted heartbeats
    yitgadal
blackened air
    veyitkadash
suffocating silence
    shm'ei raba
while Your clouds
    b'alma
drift
    di-v'ra
beyond the chimneys
    khirutei
but there is no dawn
    v'yamlikh
over Auschwitz
    malkhutei
and having ignored the fire
    b'khayeikhon
denied its smoke
    uv'yomeikhon
forgotten the numbers
    uv'khayei
on their arms
    d'khol beit yisroel
You remain alone
    Ba'agala
forever covered
    uvizman kariv

by ashes
   v'imru amen

see the little children cry
      see their tears
      watch them die
never will their faces fade
      from Your shattered eyes

Psalm 13, Post-Auschwitz

You hid Your face
ignored Your world
while flesh-fueled flames pierced the sky
ashes not dew covered Your mornings
dying children saw Your back
did not hear Your voice

they trusted in Your faithfulness
even as they entered
Your final sanctuary
even as they inhaled
your poisoned breath
even as they began
to sleep the sleep of death

You can never restore luster to their eyes
and I no longer wait for Your deliverance

it is too late

Birkenau Barracks

cold wind blows
through crumbling barrack walls
rotted wood soaked with
vomit
blood
rain
dew
cracking under the sun
dust covering ashes in unswept corners

they remain defiant, the barracks
as ice wind blows
past flames no longer burning
now without screams
without shadows
not even echoed whispers

so let them stand guard, the barracks
rows of tombstones
for faceless hallucinations
disintegrating into their corpses' earth
leaving only frozen wind
to mourn

death was

death was reflection
of smoke expanding outward
against its own blackness

death was sanctuary
from imagined whispers
shadows
beyond flames
beyond the sky

death was memory
of one flower
rooted in not yet dried blood
still blooming through barbed wire

death is reflection
of itself
sanctuary
from itself
memory
into itself

death is not
evil

ora pro nobis

Birkenau Nocturne

a psalm for the destruction
out of moss-covered rubble
between pillars of colorless ashes
and wild flowers
burning voices rise
in a blood-jagged rainbow
to remind
You
Who allowed today's amalekites
to take days from Your children's days
centuries from generations
of Your broken oath

Sosnowiec Visited

light cuts the rain grey
semi-darkness
through curtains
sixty years old

from across the street
that should have been
but never will be
mine
I see shadows move
behind windows where
another family once lived
same rooms
same walls
same bricks
perhaps even the same furniture

here the good church-going citizens
watched and waited
until the non-believers
the non-Poles
were finally taken away,
then they stole
my mother's home
her bed
her clothes
my brother's toys

dead Jew reborn
to refuse to knock on their door
any door
I came to curse
only to find
them cursed already

my final victory: I can leave

even the air tastes bitter

Thunder Burial

Thunder burial before dawn in the
damp, lead-grey Treblinka darkness,
and even God is condemned to pray
whispers in Her own penultimate
nightmare of charred hallucinations,
but backwards, forever backwards,
to No One

the difference

the difference
between John Smith
and
Hans Schmidt
is that I never wonder
whether John's father
killed my brother

At Belsen

enter a realm
ruled only
by earth
dried grass
which do not conceal
unhidden graves

eyes closed
think of the child
that was
but never
became;
remember them
walking
in the gray wind
under freezing suns;
feel the blood
that would not burn
will not disappear
invisibly soaking
spreading

one stone
above the bones:
lonely vigil
mute prophet
ever prosecutor

try to cry
without tears;
scream
in silence;
mourn
but not wallow

why return?

the dead refuse
to leave

Crematory Smoke

before Auschwitz
God created man
and before man
Himself
and then He became fire
leaving only fear
of His ashes
to rule the emptiness

and as the ovens
began defiling their corpses
fire also died
only to be replaced
by other flames

Lamentations

in memory of Benjamin, my brother

and even if a million dying children
did not destroy Creation
there will be another
almost forgotten
universe
over which God will have to cry
those tears
that should have extinguished
the fires of Auschwitz

Kol Nidre in Bergen-Belsen

for my father

twice murdered shadows
rising slowly
out of deserted
almost forgotten
mass graves
walking naked
through smoke
no longer breathable air
death fog
in the stone covered silence
of mankind's forever frozen
ashes
nameless
faceless
holier than God
unprayed to

Montage

years faded by
    calm days erase the night
        new flowers on their graves

snow without blood
    forgotten burning ashes
        hidden reminders buried

sunshines now warm
    unwritten names stay lost
        brothers embrace

prayers have dried
    white tombstones smile
        rivers recrossed

eyes change
    winds cease to talk
        words grow again

and yet I cannot listen to a German song

East Upper Silesia from Above

pure snow on other lands
other fields
other trees
reflect sunrise
not here
fog colors dominate
ice furrows reek vomit
soot roads lead
to themselves
into themselves
choking the mind numb
a different death

Midnight Hallucinations

ghost children paint
black butterflies
against burning flowers
as my grandfather's eyes
transcend eternity
to remind me why
I bear his name

First Flame

having sparked the first flame
Creator of not being
of blackness before and after light
You may not disavow
unburied ashes
of Your only lie

Warsaw Trees

naked branches slash jagged
across lead morning sky
raw bones extend
from to be resurrected corpses
above earth blood long ago abandoned
as slav laughter
not quite aryan but close enough
still echoes atonally
through ice-swept sanctuaries where
unlike Moriah
God refused to speak

Yizkor

you whose eyes knew mine
in that contaminated paradise
of vomit soup and black potato peels
do not intone
God's Kaddish
for my name
but mourn me only
as a faceless number
carved
into nocturnal ashes

Morning Prologue

to reawaken from treblinka's
unlit darklessness:
>a self-reflected mirror image
>shadowed against its annihilated
>now
>in the still noxious
>decomposing
>stench
>of *kölnischwasser 4711*
>>and
>>zyklon b

Tishah b'Av, 1943

perhaps a sudden
unresisting
silence
or merely God
exiled
into phantasmal
cosmic solitude
on this the endless Ninth Day
of Her final Av

They Wait

forgotten on roads rebuilt with ashes
they wait
child ghosts of twilight
humming voiceless melodies
last heard accompanied by
zyklon-b hiss

mary cries for her son
but not for other mothers'
sons daughters

and still they wait
child ghosts dominating
god's final requiem
against skeletal trees
in fire-sleep

jesus
voluntary sufferer
meet a five-year-old night angel
who did nothing to deserve
the agony
of dying for your sins
murdered by the blood-pure
baptized in
never ejected from
your church

and still they wait
child ghosts of whirlwinds
suffocating in darkness
after the doors slammed shut
after the air turned sour
after all prayer ceased

Agnus Dei

An infant disappeared, led
into the gas, and a flower
began to grow. A million
roses, red, one for every
child, covering the fields
while shouting to the stars:
No, we are not yet dead.

Ne'ilah

alone
abandoned in silent blackness
my brother's child shadow
fades gently
too gently
against time-frozen flames
into never

Teutonic Renewal

look at the mountains
where flowers never stopped growing
look at the highways
rebuilt better than before
look at all the new mausoleums
of shining glass and steel
look at the policemen
whose fathers were policemen
and are now drinking
the same beer
look at forests
which remain untorched
and then tell me
apollyon's rabble
gray-haired gray-faced bankers
have not won

Wiedergutmachung

the Aryan bureaucrats
post-Nazi, of course
and very polite
in their dignified
Berlin Frankfurt Hamburg offices
would like all survivors to die
at least disappear
now
so they can stop pretending
that they have regrets

"we've paid too much already"
"it's not our fault"
"it wasn't us"
"oh, if we'd only won the war"

they have learned to torture
most efficiently
by antiseptic memorandum
"application denied"
"you filed too late"
"insufficient documentation"
"you didn't suffer enough"
"you didn't fill out the right forms"
and grin each time they see
"payee deceased"
on returned checks
"this Jew won't bother us again"
"it took him long enough"
"please have a glass of schnapps"

their fathers would be proud

you are not heroes

you are not heroes
you are not righteous

you watched
perhaps some of you looked away
as the undesirables
the non-poles
the non-christians
were led away

you watched
as your neighbors
perhaps your friends
who prayed in your church
extorted
betrayed
raped
urged the killers
to kill

when they were gone
you stole their homes
violated their beds
threw away their books
in languages you could not read
with the garbage

how does this make you heroes?
how does it make you righteous?

yes, we know there were those
who hid

who rescued
who imperiled their lives
but they were far too few

and anyway
they were not you

"why are you still alive?"
you asked the few ghosts
who dared to return
"who gave you the right
"to remind us
"who we are
"what we are?"

we honor those
who stood with us then
who stand with us today

but you
who watched in silence then
and who today
defend
deny
the scavengers who preyed
on still living carcasses

you are not heroes
you are not righteous

animarum vestrarum misereatur deus

Knit Doll at Bergen-Belsen

the little girl
hugs her knit doll
tight to her chest
kisses it
whispers to it
cries into it

dull white
brown wool for
hair
shoes
the doll is all
she has left
from before
hunger
cold
typhus
dirt
watered-down turnip soup

the little girl
hugs her knit doll
as she plays
among corpses

Mute Lamentations

We, the last children
    of this december age
    stand alone without hope
    on yesterday's snow-covered
    ashes
    while invisible fire-angels
    still redden
    the windless midnight air
    of man's self-crucifixion
    and god is finally forced to hear
    our eternal henceforth unanswerable
    questions:
                where
                if not here
                is your grave
                and when
                if not now
                is infinity?

stop preaching

stop preaching
that murderers didn't kill
that erstwhile friends
didn't betray
that cowards
didn't rape
that cold eyes
didn't watch
the almost dead
the not yet dead
led away
that grinning neighbors
didn't steal
that hovering vultures
didn't extort
that church-taught hatred
wasn't there

blood once shed
can never be
unshed

Meditation

the miracle
after god did not respond
to cries from the depths
of auschwitz
is that jews
continue to pray
despite auschwitz

Treblinka

The tree that stood and watched me die
    still waits beneath a clouded sky,
    still sees a fading corpse walk by,
and still forbids its birds to fly.

The wind I met that summer day
    still hears the words a ghost must say,
    still echoes sounds which cannot stay,
and still blows ashes from the way.

The frozen earth in which I lie
    still feels the blood that will not dry,
    still lets the faceless infant cry,
and still won't cease to ask God why?

But I who do not own a name
    still know that man remains the same,
    still look into one blinding flame,
and still fear nights that never came.

Beyond Ashes

in vain they look
to the once holy mountain
now barren
as fires god forgot
burn through rain
burn the rain
and monotonous prayers
wither into noxious night
for beyond ashes
there is no redemption

Yad Vashem Museum Opening

cool wind blowing colder
becoming ice
sun fading into darkness
under Judean clouds
grey against black
we sit shivering in our
coats
hats
woolen socks
knowing that
coffee
brandy
a warm bed
are only an hour or two away

cold winds blew colder
became ice
sun fading into darkness
grey clouds against black
there
sixty years before
shivering in drafty barracks
praying for death as respite
from hunger
from pain
from tomorrow's hunger
tomorrow's pain

images I never saw
but remembered from words
whispers
of the almost murdered
now etched forever
inside a hill
where my daughter
will walk through shadows
know reflections
hear echoes
of her grandparents' memories
fading
dark grey against black
as cool winds blow colder
becoming ice
under the Jerusalem sun

Auschwitz-Birkenau, January 27, 2015

no longer visible flames
still burn
will always burn
have burned my brother's tiny body
for seventy-one years
five months, twenty-three days
since he became only a memory
my, our mother's memory
now my inheritance
in a huge tent we sit
three thousand of us
and I see where
my mother was unable to kiss
her child
one last time
I cannot feel him shiver
I cannot hear him cry
I cannot smell the gas
perhaps I am breathing
his ashes

The Second Generation

true, we are the children
of a nocturnal twilight
the heirs of Auschwitz and Ponar
but ours is also the rainbow
in us the storm meets sunlight
to create new colors
as we add defiant sparks
to an eternal fire

a second through the air

a second through the air
maybe two
into the night
away from the train
toward the river
and then the bullets hit
arm
leg
forehead
he no longer feels
no longer hears
until the water jolts him awake
cradles him
forces him to return
he does not remember what he saw
whom he saw
beyond
but knows
that he cannot stay
that he must go on
that he must go back

Father

I used to be a part of you
belong to you
the extension of your being
but now
you live within me
are the spark
of my consciousness

I say kaddish for you
            with you
            as you
sing your melodies
speak your words
hearing your voice in mine
and my eyes
too green
have somehow started to reflect
the blue of yours

I used to be a part of you
protected by your presence
by your light
but now
the time is mine
and alone
I must be more than myself
your son
has become your heir
has become you

two broken candles

two broken candles
carved into grey stone
for Devora
Yaacov's daughter
Mendel's wife
in the haunted
haunting
Czeladź cemetery

thousands of graves
one next to
the second
next to
the third
row
after row
after row

once wives and husbands
sons and daughters
friends and cousins
came here to talk with those
who cannot leave
no more
now the dead speak only
to each other
and my grandmother's stone
with its two broken candles
waits for me to stand
where my father stood
with his father
to pray and cry
where he prayed and cried
as a child

as a man
before the whirlwind

did I rest my head
where he once placed his?
did he whisper to me
or was it the summer wind?
nothing else is left
of a family
my family
all others vanished
remains desecrated
ashes scattered
only this grey stone
above my grandmother's grave
with its two broken candles

voiceless melodies

for Jodi

voiceless melodies drift forgotten
through their fog-imbued vacuum
of invisible sparks
above God's eternal twilight
only to be heard
transcending heaven
at the birth of a child

Yearnings for My Father

return to me in unannounced dreams
to fill my heart
each time forever
with ethereal hopes
of being together again

blessed is the soul

in memory of my mother

blessed is the soul
that lit smoke-choked darkness
from within
defying
defeating
death's shadows

blessed is the soul
that watched her own son
fade into ashes
and still sheltered
the weak
the abandoned
the sick
above all
the children

blessed is the soul
that shattered silence
confronting
frozen nocturnal eyes
at the first dawn
of reborn justice

blessed is the soul
that emerged
from Auschwitz and Bergen-Belsen
to create hope
not tears
to teach life
not sorrow

blessed is the soul
that left us richer for her having been
but with an aching void
where divine sparks
will never again radiate
in the gentlest of smiles

blessed is her soul

night fragments

night fragments created
in fire shadows
we are the last and the first:
the last to taste ashes
from the cursed century's valley
of unwilling passers through
where God revealed His face
to them alone;
and the first
transfixed by still burning yesterdays
to reach beyond heaven and its clouds
beyond crimson ghost illusions
into ourselves
imploding
in search of memory

Kaddish Memories of My Mother

I do remember mornings
just the two of us
that last summer
you drinking tea
I coffee
talking about everything
except what we both knew was coming
what made us both so afraid
you did not understand
could not understand
your body's betrayal
wanted desperately
to be yourself again
with tears in your eyes
dread in my heart
we created illusions
as your face slowly became smaller
your voice less clear
but always your smile
from my childhood
warming away darkness
I do remember those mornings
hope they eased your anguish
wish we could live them again

A Legacy of Whispers

for Jodi on her 20th birthday

my father never gave me
his blessing
our eyes had no time
to say goodbye

I do not want
my breath to stop
my thoughts to fade
before you receive
this legacy of whispers
from my heart

no longer small
no longer weak
what can I tell you
that you do not
already know?
what can I show you
that you will not learn
on your own?

but as you grow
remember
only the fire within you
matters

so reach
not for lost stars
but for the highest branches
far above your head
alive with shadows
you alone can see;
snow-covered mountains
cutting through their fog
must be your goal
especially in rain-filled
midnight darkness;
do not look only to the sky
its blue is distance
without depth
while ocean colors
cover worlds still pure
as at the twilight
of the fifth day;
continue dreaming
as sparks of each new sunrise
fill your soul;
and never let a drifting leaf
fall to the ground
for like a breaking wave
it too reflects
creation in infinity

St. Thomas Cycle

for Jeanie

I.

drifting the eagle
black
wings burning
against a pale sky
hued by volcanic ashes
carves his reflection
invisible but to eyes closed
against horizon-edged
water mirrors

II.

gateless beach sanctuary
with time suspended in its own infinity
rain merges into sunrays
just long enough
to claim another victory
and winds carry whispers
beyond memory
here God is the stranger
unrecognized
come to experience
dusk palms

III.

go prophesy, Cassandra of the night
tell colors to emerge
first gently then erupting from the sea
tell waves
their crashing may not cease
tell clouds
to fade into themselves
tell storms
their rage will not be forgotten
by the sand
go prophesy, Cassandra of the night
dead flowers are your only audience
cragged broken shells your chorus
and the atonal sonata
of one unseen bird
creation defying nature
must force even you
to say amen
not to prayer
but to love

Royal Hotel, San Remo, July 2000

and so it was that death returned
one summer afternoon
disguised as air
perhaps a breeze
the sun reflecting
off trees
stone steps
that have known me since childhood
whose memories envelop me

second window from the end
second floor
the long balcony from which
he used to feed the birds with breakfast rolls
more than he ever ate
used to watch me
watch over me
wave to me
used to look out over the sea
into his past
my father

for forty-five years
she walked down these steps
slowly
always smiling
always regal
sat in the shade
watching me learn to swim
in the salt-water pool
watching me swim with him
swim alone
swim with her granddaughter
decades apart

always remembering
my mother

here Jeanie was a teenager
then a bride
then herself a mother
collecting lavender

here we held Jodi
as a little girl
my father always
invisibly watching
now they both watch her
walk past the trees
down the steps
our steps
theirs

shadows are the dead
time does not matter
ghosts never age
nor death

paradise comes in different forms
we each have our own
if we can find it
mine is here
in fleeting impressions
that seem to wave
seem to watch
seem to smile
that no one else can see

and so it was that death returned
not as a curse
but comforting in silent whispers
disguised
perhaps as a six o'clock cloud
green, purple and pink at its edges
warm against the cooling sky
allowing me
while here
not to be an orphan
and when I leave again
not to let go

Hallie and Jacob

your smiles have sparks
of yesterday's fires
as you search in rainbows
for colors not yet known
perhaps my parents kissed you
like they once kissed me
like my mother kissed your mother
before sending you
to become who you are
to be who you will be

Footsteps

Footsteps. Hitting the concrete sidewalk
with unbroken regularity. In the night,
their sound drifts up, explodes, but remains.
One, another, and still another, each is replaced and
destroyed in turn. Hearing nothing else,
he follows.

Footsteps. Down the empty street. A crowded
cellar. Others are there, but not really, wearing masks,
bodies in a universe of their own that he cannot touch.
Talking, drinking, laughing, dancing. Lights, dim, colored,
unreal, absurd. What is he doing there? Who wants him there?

Oh yes, some come up to him. He approaches others. A girl
he met before agrees to dance with him. Indifference. He barely
feels her hand on his shoulder. The music over, they stand.
Embarrassing silence. Polite excuses. Someone else takes her
to the dancefloor. Dim lights, colored, unreal. No one sees him
leave.

Footsteps. Hollow. Monotonous. Without variation.
Fresh air. A biting wind. Which way? Does it matter?
Both hands deep inside his pockets, he walks. Before
crossing the road, his eyes look around. No cars. A pity.
He talks to no one. And talking to no one is talking to
no one, not even to himself.

Footsteps. Empty repetition lasting long after the
end of the actual movement. He reaches what he
thinks of as his home. The room is warm, too warm.
He opens the window. Now it is too cold.

Footsteps continue into his dream. So does his search.
His name is not important. He himself forgets.

Easter Crocus

and now what child
can the Madonna
cradle
in her arms?
whose hair
can she caress?

three crosses stand
alone
near the city of david
in the hills of judaea

their earth
becomes damp;
the wood
is old;
the nails
must rust

men pray
women cry
children look

but she

she does not know
a god
nor
a savior
nor
a corpse

she only sees
her son

Christmas Eve and Winter Lanterns

Come my friends. The world
has ceased to exist, and we
are all invited to its
funeral. Tonight, men and women
are too busy praying with their
past to notice a hungry blue-eyed
little boy who would perhaps also
like to smile. A star might be
shining somewhere, but not for
the child, and no one is awake to
see it fading away into fiction.

Young man, shouts the
angry ghost, you are naïve
if you can still believe
in miracles. I try to explain
God, and he laughs; then
I speak about a flower. Even he
begins to listen.

No, I was wrong. It is
only the blue-eyed little
boy, and there will be
no funeral.

Rain Mornings

once meaningful biblical verse
and misspelled graffiti
jointly desecrate
a crumbling cemetery wall
while the abandoned dead
speak only
to bored pre-dawn pigeons
and dandelions

Messianic Shadows

twice the messiah came to earth
and twice he left in silence
unrecognized
except by a blind child
who held his hand while dreaming
about the color
of his eyes

Genesis, Post Scriptum

and on the eighth day
the devil became master
of the universe
by creating man's soul
in God's image

Refugee

echoes of exploding bombs
and blood-stained walls
cannot persuade a homeless child
that peace has come

I Believe

yes, I believe that
Jesus was God's child:
one son—not The,
nor His eldest,
nor His heir;
and murdering a man
is still a greater crime
than deicide

strange days follow wartime

strange days follow wartime
when the victor dies unmourned
of self-inflicted wounds
and the assassin fails to see
his own reflection
in the slowly drying blood

Intermezzo

not writing for years
only means
that words ferment
foment
captive in unexplored catacombs
until they release themselves
in sudden bursts of being
as burning scars
where others almost healed

The Messiah Will Not Come

the messiah will not come
God will not leave
Her seclusion
until Jerusalem's bearded
rabbis imams priests
teach daily that each
Jewish child
Palestinian infant
is created with one
only one
always the same
divine spark

False Friendship

a friend
who discards
a friend
has never been
a friend

Shadows of a Moon Unseen

for David and Romy

darkness is absolute
only when it becomes
absolute
until then
its greyness allows midnight waves
to reflect sporadic shadows
of a moon unseen
against themselves
elusive reminders that light
even the beginning of sunrise
may yet appear

Before the End

smiles and laughter
inexorably fade
into anguished awareness
that they will never again be
what they used to be
and fear of the known
becomes greater
than fear of the unknown

tomorrow

tomorrow
seeing another sunrise
light years away
phantasmagoric illusion
delusion
until sleepless night
fades into a new
greyness
and still breathing corpses
begin to anguish about
tomorrow

On Manhattan's East River Esplanade

for Robbie

flaming red
early morning sun
against God's cerulean sky
piercing deep below the water
through stray clouds
faster than walking
not quite running
lost in Beethoven's penultimate string quartet
allegro ma non troppo
cool wind in my face
strangers jogging toward me
past me
and for a moment I forget
that we are
no longer young

After Genocide

for Adisada

ghosts of murdered men
boys
fathers
husbands
brothers
sons
invade refugee camp dreams
their faces fading
in a soundless
last goodbye
against gunshots
8,000 gunshots
echoing without end
and as the child waits
not knowing
her srebrenica ghosts
do not want
god
to find them
take them
from their emptiness
even though
he
already did

slow rumble thunder

slow rumble thunder
somewhere above
behind
grey clouds
blocking off a sun-drenched sky
that also needs
a day of rest

I can imagine

I can imagine
God dancing
at the birth of a child
and
I can imagine
God mourning
when one of His creations
fades away
but I cannot see
God wanting prayer
to cause illness
or death

# of course Black lives matter

for Mike

Black lives matter
of course Black lives matter
and if we want
us
any of us
to remember
Jewish lives extinguished at Auschwitz
Bosniak lives at Srebrenica
Tutsi lives in Butare
Serbian lives at Jasenovac
Armenian lives at Musa Dagh
Fur lives in Darfur
Rohingya lives in Myanmar
then we must now all shout
that Black lives matter
until no child of God
ever again dies gasping
"I can't breathe"

Glossary

Agnus Dei—Latin, "Lamb of God," Roman Catholic prayer.

Allegro ma non troppo—Italian, musical tempo mark indicating that a passage is to be played fast but not overly so

Animarum vestrarum misereatur deus—Latin, "God have mercy on your souls."

Auschwitz-Birkenau—the largest and most notorious of the Nazi German death camps located in German-occupied Poland.

Baruch Atah Adonai Eloheinu—Hebrew, "Blessed are You, our Lord, our God."

Bergen-Belsen—Nazi concentration camp in Germany that became a Displaced Persons camp for five years after the end of World War II.

"I can't breathe"—last words uttered by George Floyd as he was being killed by a white police officer in Minneapolis, Minnesota, on May 25, 2020, in what World Jewish Congress President Ronald S. Lauder denounced as a "horrific racist act."

Kaddish—Jewish mourners' prayer, a sanctification of God.

Kol Nidre—"All Vows," Aramaic prayer sung at the beginning of services on the eve of Yom Kippur, the Jewish Day of Atonement.

Kölnischwasser 4711—Brand of perfume manufactured in the German city of Cologne since at least 1799.

Ne'ilah—the concluding service on Yom Kippur.

Ora pro nobis—Latin, "pray for us."

Srebrenica—town in eastern Bosnia where Bosnian Serb forces perpetrated a genocide in July 1995 by murdering approximately 8,000 Bosniak—that is, Bosnian Muslim—men and boys and deporting more than 25,000 Bosniak women children and elderly men.

Tishah b'Av—the ninth day of the Hebrew month of Av, a Jewish communal fast day marking the destruction of the First and Second Temples in Jerusalem in 587/586 B.C.E and 70 C.E. respectively, as well as other disasters that befell the Jewish people throughout history.

Treblinka—Nazi German death camp located in German-occupied Poland.

Wiedergutmachung—German, reparations, literally, "to make good again."

Yad Vashem—Israel's national institution for the remembrance of the Holocaust.

Yizkor—Hebrew, "Remember," Jewish memorial service.

Zyklon B—Toxic gas used in the gas chambers of the Nazi German death camps.

About the Author

Born in the Displaced Persons camp of Bergen-Belsen in Germany, Menachem Z. Rosensaft is Associate Executive Vice President and General Counsel of the World Jewish Congress, and teaches about the law of genocide at the law schools of Columbia and Cornell Universities. He holds an M.A. degree from The Writing Seminars at Johns Hopkins University, received together with his B.A. from Johns Hopkins; an M.A. in modern European history from Columbia University; and a J.D. from Columbia Law School. He is the founding chairman of the International Network of Children of Jewish Holocaust Survivors, a past president of Park Avenue Synagogue in New York City, and serves on the Advisory Council of the Foundation for Memorial Sites in Lower Saxony, Germany. He was appointed to the United States Holocaust Memorial Council by Presidents Bill Clinton and Barack Obama. Menachem is the editor of *The World Jewish Congress, 1936-2016* (WJC, 2017), *God, Faith & Identity from the Ashes: Reflections of Children and Grandchildren of Holocaust Survivors* (Jewish Lights Publishing, 2015), and *Life Reborn, Jewish Displaced Persons 1945-1951* (U.S. Holocaust Memorial Museum, 2001), and co-author, with his daughter, Jodi Rosensaft, of "A Measure of Justice: The Early History of German-Jewish Reparations," published as an Occasional Paper by the Leo Baeck Institute (2003).

Kelsay Books